Hattie

As the Cr

Music and Lyrics

GW00391622

Bloomsbury Methuen Drama
An imprint of Bloomsbury Publishing Plc

B L O O M S B U R Y
LONDON • OXFORD • NEW YORK • NEW DELHI • SYDNEY

Bloomsbury Methuen Drama

An imprint of Bloomsbury Publishing Plc

Imprint previously known as Methuen Drama

50 Bedford Square	1385 Broadway
London	New York
WC1B 3DP	NY 10018
UK	USA

www.bloomsbury.com

BLOOMSBURY, METHUEN DRAMA and the Diana logo are trademarks of Bloomsbury Publishing Plc

First published 2017

British Library Cataloguing-in-Publication Data
A catalogue record for this book is available from the British Library.

ISBN: PB: 978-1-3500-4245-2
ePDF: 978-1-3500-4242-1
ePub: 978-1-3500-4243-8

Library of Congress Cataloging-in-Publication Data
A catalog record for this book is available from the Library of Congress

Cover design: Olivia D'Cruz
Cover image: Crow © Bliznetsov / Landscape © fotoVoyager

Series: Modern Plays

Typeset by Mark Heslington Ltd, Scarborough, North Yorkshire
Printed and bound in Great Britain

To find out more about our authors and books visit *www.bloomsbury.com*. Here you will find extracts, author interviews, details of forthcoming events and the option to sign up for our *newsletters*.

PENTABUS
RURAL THEATRE COMPANY

SALISBURY PLAYHOUSE

A Pentabus Theatre Company and
Salisbury Playhouse Production

As the Crow Flies

By Hattie Naylor

Music and Lyrics by Dom Coyote

Supported using public funding by
**ARTS COUNCIL
ENGLAND**

LOTTERY FUNDED

PENTABUS
RURAL THEATRE COMPANY

We are the nation's rural theatre company.

We develop, produce and tour new plays to village halls, fields, communities and theatres telling stories with local relevance and national impact.

Since 1974 Pentabus has produced 160 new plays, supported 100 playwrights and reached nearly a million audience members. We've won awards, pioneered live-streaming and continue to nurture young writers from rural backgrounds.

Our plans for the future will see us tour to new far-flung rural communities, work with new and established artists and playwrights, extend our young writers' programme and continue to push at the boundaries of what theatre can be.

Pentabus is a registered charity (number 287909). We rely on the generosity of our donors, small and large.

Brilliant new theatre, made in the countryside.

You can find out more about us at *www.pentabus.co.uk*

Twitter @pentabustheatre

Facebook Pentabus Theatre

Artistic Director	Sophie Motley
Managing Director	Kitty Ross
Development Manager	Francesca Opiekornoll
Producer	Jenny Pearce
Audience Development & Marketing	Crayg Ward
Technical Manager	Sam Eccles
Bookkeeper	Lynda Lynne
Associate Artists	Simon Longman, Michael Quartey
Volunteers	Mike Price, Stephen Abbott

Pentabus Theatre Company, Bromfield, Ludlow, Shropshire, SY8 2JU

Pentabus is also supported by The Millichope Foundation

SALISBURY PLAYHOUSE

Salisbury Playhouse is an arts and educational charity and one of Britain's leading producing theatres, with a national reputation for home-grown work of the highest quality that attracts audiences from across Wiltshire, Hampshire, Dorset and beyond.

The building comprises the 517-seat Main House, the 149-seat Salberg, a purpose-built Rehearsal Room and Community and Education Room. There is also an on-site scenery workshop, wardrobe and props store.

In addition to producing its own productions and welcoming the UK's leading touring companies, Salisbury Playhouse's extensive Take Part programme engages with more than 14,000 people of all ages each year, offering a range of creative learning, community and youth theatre activities.

Since being launched in 2014, Salisbury Playhouse's Original Drama programme included *The Magna Carta Plays, Clause 39, This Land* (produced with Pentabus Theatre Company), *Bike* and *Up Down Man* (produced with Myrtle Theatre Company). 2017 sees the return of *Worst Wedding Ever* by Chris Chibnall (produced with the New Wolsey Theatre Ipswich and Queen's Theatre Hornchurch) and *Echo's End* by Barney Norris.

Artistic Director Gareth Machin

Executive Director Sebastian Warrack

www.salisburyplayhouse.com

Tour Dates 2017

7 March | Bromfield Village Hall | Shropshire

8 March | Bromfield Village Hall | Shropshire

9 March | All Stretton Village Hall | Shropshire

10 March | Heightington Village Hall | Worcestershire

11 March | Wyre Piddle Village Hall | Worcestershire

16 March | Hereford College | Herefordshire

17 March | Neston Town Hall | Cheshire

18 March | Gawsworth Village Hall | Cheshire

19 March | Plumley Vilage Hall | Cheshire

22 March | Ketteringham Village Hall | Norfolk

23 March | Cley Marshes Visitor Centre | Norfolk

24 March | Wortwell Community Centre | Norfolk

25 March | Freckenham Village Hall | Norfolk

28 March – 8 April | The Salberg, Salisbury Playhouse | Wiltshire

12 April | Trowbridge Arts | Wiltshire

13 April | Chilmark Village Hall | Wiltshire

14 April | Newton Tony Memorial Hall | Wiltshire

15 April | Somerford's Walter Powell Primary School | Wiltshire

20 April | West Anstey Village Hall | Devon

21 April | North Molton Victory Hall | Devon

22 April | Atherington Pavilion | Devon

26 April | Heanor Baptist Church | Derbyshire

27 April | Terry O'Toole Theatre | Lincolnshire

28 April | Thrumpton Village Hall | Nottinghamshire

29 April | Clent Parish Hall | Worcestershire

30 April | Leintwardine Community Centre | Herefordshire

As the Crow Flies was first performed at Bromfield Village Hall, Shropshire, on Tuesday 7 March 2017 with the following cast and creative team:

Cast

Tom Brownlee
Natalia Campbell
Imelda Warren-Green

Creative team

Writer	Hattie Naylor
Director	Elizabeth Freestone
Designer	Carla Goodman
Composer & Musical Director	Dom Coyote
Lighting Designer	James Mackenzie
Movement Director	Kitty Winter
Production Manager	Tammy Rose
Technical Manager	Sam Eccles
Touring Stage Manager	Oran O'Neill

Special thanks to: A.C Lighting, John, Chris and Julia from Live & Local, the NRTF, Sakuntala Ramanee, Fionn Gill, Beatrice Curnew, Richard Coen, Pam Yarwood, Eleanor Creed-Miles, David Howe, Tim Brewer, Mark Ferreo, Cuan Wildlife Rescue and Vale Wildlife Hospital and Rehabilitation Centre

Developed in conjunction with a group of volunteer promoters as part of the Live & Local DART Scheme

CAST

Tom Brownlee | Alfie

Tom trained at the Royal Welsh College of Music and Drama.

His theatre credits include: *Across The Dark Water* (Berry Theatre); *Romeo and Juliet*, *The Talented Mr Ripley* and *Joan of Arc* (The Faction); *Woman of Flowers* and *Anne of Green Gables* (Forest Forge); *You Once Said Yes* (Look Left Look Right); *Alice and Victor* (BLOCKseventeen); *Stand Up Diggers All* (Pentabus Theatre @ Latitude Festival); *The Woman in White* (Lincoln Theatre Royal and UK tour); *Antony and Cleopatra, Shelter, Blitz* and *Blood on the Laboratory Floor* (Nuffield Theatre); *Romeo and Juliet* (Ludlow Festival/Exeter Northcott Theatre) and *She Stoops to Conquer* (Birmingham Rep and UK tour).

Television: *Doctors* (BBC).

Voice: *Space Play* (Brave Badger Theatre); *The Great War Reminiscences of Private Ginger Byrne* (BBC Online); *The Crusade in Jeans* (Kasander Film Company); *Romeo and Juliet* – The Anniversary Song (David Snasdell Ltd) and various English Language Tape Productions with Pearson Education Ltd.

Tom's voice also appears at *www.damngoodvoices.com*

Natalia Campbell | Beth

Natalia trained at Lee Strasberg Studio, Middlesex University and Barking College.

Her most recent work includes: *Little Red and the Big Bad Wolf* (Unity Theatre Liverpool and Action Transport Theatre); *The Hobbit* (The Dukes, Lancaster); *The Iranian Feast* and *It's a Wonderful Life* (Farnham Maltings); *Medea* (Actors of Dionysus); *The Wife of Bath* and *Harlequin Goes to the Moon* (The Rude Mechanicals); *The Oresteia* (The Steam Industry); *Littlest Quirky* (Theatre Centre); *Exile* (Theatre503); *The Fortune Club, The Wind and the Wash Tub, Palace of Fear* and *Bollywood Jane* (Leicester Haymarket); *Starfish* (Theatremongers); *Taj* (Big Picture Company); *The Hunchback of Notre Dame* and *Arabian Nights* (OTTC) and *Ten Tiny Fingers, Nine Tiny Toes* (Firefly Productions).

Natalia also spent six years touring twenty-five countries with TNT/ADG Theatre, spanning Europe, Asia, Central America and the Middle East, appearing as Beatrice in *Much Ado About Nothing*,

Emilia and Bianca in *Othello*, Nurse in *Romeo and Juliet*, Gertrude in *Hamlet*, Titania and Hippolyta in *A Midsummer Night's Dream* and Kate in *The Taming of the Shrew*. Highlights of her tours included performing at the copy of the Globe in Tokyo, the foothills of the Himalayas and being part of the first Western theatre company to perform Shakespeare in Vietnam and at the National Theatre of China in Beijing.

Her site-specific work includes: *The Grand Hotel Budapest* and *Back to the Future* (Secret Cinema); *Emergency Exit Arts* (Colossus Awake & Return); *Heartbreak Hotel* (The Jetty); *Oedipus* (Gods and Monsters); *Baited Hooks* (Clio's Company); *Medea* (Actors of Dionysus) and *Project Dream* – Wildness Festival and Wellcome Collection (Contemporary Vintage).

Her vocal and dance work includes: *Treasure Island* (Tramshed Theatre); *Little Boots* (music video); *Cinderella* (Hiss & Boo); *Jungle Book* and *Ali Baba* (U.S.E); *Nothing But Dreams* (Musical Futures – Greenwich Theatre); Castrol Oil (advert); Gemma Hayes (music video); *Jambalaya* (music video); *Mulan* (Walt Disney); DJ Ritu (UK and Spanish tour) and Tango Argumentio (Flying Gorillas).

Her screen work includes: *EastEnders*, *Casualty*, *Modern Manners*, *One-day* (BBC); *Duelling Women*, *Show Me Something Different*, *Learn to Love* (short films) as well as other work for Discovery Channel, ITV and SKY.

To find out more visit *www.nataliacampbell.com*

Imelda Warren-Green | Young Beth

Imelda graduated from Mountview Academy of Theatre Arts with a first class honours degree in Musical Theatre.

Credits include: Step sister in *Cinderella* (Chiswick Gardens pop-up theatre); Jamie Pack in *Out There* (Union Theatre); Denny Blood in *Bad Girls* (Union Theatre); Miriam in *Nativity Blues* (Eastern Angles Theatre Company); Nan in *Whistle Down the Wind* (Union Theatre). Workshops include: Lisa in *The Train on Platform 1* (Eastern Angles Theatre Company). Credits whilst training: Anna in Leo Tolstoy's *Anna Karenina*, Ilse in *Spring Awakening* and Beggar Woman in *Sweeney Todd*.

CREATIVE TEAM

Hattie Naylor | Writer

Hattie Naylor's credits include: *Ivan And the Dogs*, *The Night Watch*, *Going Dark*, *Clause 39*, and *Bluebeard*. *Ivan and the Dogs* (Soho Theatre and ATC), was nominated in the Olivier Awards for Outstanding Achievement in Theatre, won the Tinniswood Award in 2010, and has been performed to further acclaim internationally. Further productions include: *Weighting*, with the partially disabled circus/theatre company Extraordinary Bodies (national tour 2015/16), and *The Night Watch*, her adaptation of Sarah Waters' novel (Manchester Royal Exchange), was listed as one of the top theatre plays of the year for 2016 by The Observer. *Going Dark* was co-written and created with Sound&Fury (Young Vic and Science Museum 2013/14 and national tour), and her controversial *Bluebeard* was directed by Lee Lyford and created by their own company Gallivant (Soho Theatre and national tour 2013). Further credits include: *Moominland Midwinter* with The Egg Theatre and Horse and Bamboo (2013), and *The Nutcracker* with Paul Dodgson for Theatre Royal Bath (2009) both directed by Lee Lyford. Her work as a librettist includes *Picard in Space* with Will Gregory (Goldfrapp), directed by Jude Kelly, for the Electronica Festival at the South Bank (2012). She has written extensively for BBC Radio 4, notably *The Diaries of Samuel Pepys* (nominated Best Radio Drama 2012), *The Aeneid* (nominated Best Radio Adaptation, BBC Audio Awards 2013), *How to Survive the Roman Empire* and *The Letters of Pliny* (2016).

Work in development includes: a feature film of *Ivan And the Dogs* with Salon Pictures and the film director Andrew Kötting (*Gallivant*, *Swandown*), *Yana* with Pickled Image, and *Bluebeard* with Teatro di Roma.

Hattie currently teaches scriptwriting at Sheffield Hallam University.

Elizabeth Freestone | Director

Elizabeth is a freelance theatre director whose credits include: *The Rape of Lucrece*, *Here Lies Mary Spindler*, *The Tragedy of Thomas Hobbes* and *The Comedy of Errors* (RSC); *Endless Light* (Kali/Southwark Playhouse); *The Duchess of Malfi*, *Dr Faustus*, *The School for Scandal*, *Volpone* (Greenwich Theatre); *Romeo and Juliet* (Shakespeare's Globe); *The Water Harvest* (Theatre503) and *Left on Church Street* (Bridewell). She is the former Artistic Director of Pentabus for whom she directed *Here I Belong* by Matt Hartley, *From Land to Mouth* by Bethan Marlow, *The Lone Pine Club* by Alice Birch, *Milked* by Simon Longman, *Each Slow Dusk* by Rory Mullarkey, *In This Place* by Frances Brett and Lydia Adetunji, *For Once* by Tim Price, *Blue Sky* by Clare Bayley, *This Same England* with Lorraine Stanley, *Stand Up Diggers All* by Phil Porter and *The Hay Play* by Nell Leyshon.

She was the Associate Director for *A Caucasian Chalk Circle* at the National and has also worked as a Staff Director both there and at the RSC. She was an Assistant Director at the Royal Court, Soho and Hampstead. She trained at Rose Bruford College and the National Theatre Studio.

Carla Goodman | Designer

Carla trained in Nottingham, London and New York.

Recent design credits include: *Jack and the Beanstalk* (Cast); *How to Date* (Arcola Theatre); *Exposure* (St James); *Rise* (Old Vic Outdoors); *Miss Julie* (Etcetera); *Not Moses* (Arts Theatre); *Romeo and Juliet* (Orange Tree); *Pig Farm* (St James); *Heartbreak Hotel* (The Jetty, Greenwich); *Truce* (New Wimbledon Theatre); *What Flows Past the Baltic* (Nottingham Playhouse); *Theatre Uncut* (Traverse Theatre and UK tour); *Listen, We're Family* (Wilton's Music Hall); *Ariodante* (Royal Academy of Music); *Miss Nightingale* (Lowry Theatre and UK tour) and *Mush And Me* (Bush Theatre).

Upcoming work includes *Gabriel* (Richmond Theatre and UK tour) and *Pride and Prejudice* (Nottingham Playhouse).

Dom Coyote | Composer & Musical Director

Dom Coyote is a composer, performer and songwriter. He works with bands, theatre companies and arts projects across the UK and internationally. He also leads on his own projects, mixing music and theatre in unexpected ways. Dom was a member of the National Youth Theatre. He went on to study Creative Writing at Dartington College of Arts and then gained an apprenticeship with Kneehigh Theatre, who he now works with regularly. His gig-theatre show *Songs for the End of the World* won the Origins Award for outstanding achievement, Vault Festival, London, 2016.

Projects include: *The Borrowers* (Sherman Cymru); *The Story Fishers* (National Theatre); *RISE* (Old Vic); *Little Sister* (Royal Exchange); *Watership Down* (Watermill Theatre); *Cape Sound*

Stories (HKW, Berlin); *Songs for the End of the World* (Battersea Arts Centre/West Yorkshire Playhouse); *Minotaur* (Unicorn Theatre); *The Caucasian Chalk Circle* (Unicorn Theatre); *The Night Before Christmas* (West Yorkshire Playhouse); *Extraordinary Bodies* (Cirque Bijou/Diverse City); *Kes* (CAST); *Bridging the Gap* (Bristol Green Capital); Vena Portae (band, published by Domino); Folk in a Box (Sydney Festival/Venice Biennale); Talking Souls (British Council South Africa); The Impending Storm (British Council, South Africa); *The Raun Tree* (West Yorkshire Playhouse); *The Empress* (Emma Rice, RSC); *Don Jon* (Kneehigh, RSC); *A Matter of Life and Death* (Kneehigh, National Theatre) and *Cymbeline* (Kneehigh, RSC).

James Mackenzie | Lighting Designer

James trained at Rose Bruford College.

For Pentabus: *This Land* and *Milked*. Other credits include: *Machine Show* (International Dance Festival Birmingham); *Run* (2Faced Dance); *Mmm Hmm* (Verity Standen); *TEN* (Tavaziva Dance); *By the Light of the Fool Moon* (Hocket and Hoot); *Dark Wood Deep Snow* (Northern Stage); *Jason and the Argonauts* (Courtyard Theatre); *Close Distance* (Parlor Dance); *Finding Joy* (Vamos Theatre); *The Rock* and *Suitcase Story* (Dance East); *The Legend of Captain Crow's Teeth* (Unicorn Theatre); *DNA* (Hull Truck); *Macbeth* (Courtyard Theatre); *Herding Cats* (Hampstead); *See* (Company Decalage); *Shattered* (Feral Productions); *Steam* (Royal Festival Hall); *Cut it Out* (Young Vic). James is also the Artistic Director of the award winning ZOO Venues at the Edinburgh Festival Fringe.

Kitty Winter | Movement Director

Kitty Winter is a movement director, choreographer and director; she trained at Laban and on the MA Movement course at the Central School of Speech and Drama.

Recent movement credits include: *The Kite Runner* (Nottingham Playhouse/Wyndham's Theatre London); *Alice in Wonderland*, *Cinderella*, *A Christmas Carol* and *The Rise and Fall of Little Voice* (Derby Theatre); *Here I Belong* (Pentabus); *Blood* (Tamasha/Belgrade Theatre Coventry); *Rapunzel* and *Jack* (Nottingham Playhouse); *Tiny Treasures* and *The Night Pirates* (Theatre Hullabaloo); *The Dog House*, *Women on the Verge of HRT* and

Puss in Boots (Derby LIVE); *Swan Canaries* (Arletty Theatre); *The Magical Playroom* (Seabright Productions/Pleasance Edinburgh); *Roots* (Mercury Theatre Colchester); *Ghandi* and *Coconuts* (Kali Theatre/The Arcola); *Dick Turpin's Last Ride* (Theatre Royal Bury St Edmunds) and *Squid* (Theatre Royal Stratford East).

Recent directing credits include: *Feet First* and *Car Story* (Box Clever Theatre); *Spinning Yarns* and *FIVE* (Theatre Hullabaloo/Theatre Direct, Canada); *The Blue Moon* (Wriggle Dance Theatre); *Anything to Declare?* (The Gramophones); *Whose Shoes?* (Nottingham Playhouse) and *Awaking Durga* (Kali Theatre/Soho Theatre).

Kitty is Co-artistic Director of family theatre company WinterWalker, and has recently produced and directed *The Nutcracker and the Mouse King* (Lincoln Drill Hall and Déda, Derby); *Three Keepers* (UK tour); *Come to the Circus* (Déda, Derby) and *The Beast of Belper* (Belper Arts Festival). You can find out more about her work at *www.kittywinter.com*

As the Crow Flies

Cast

Beth
Alfie
Young Beth *(female, looking hippy-ish, green top/jumper and flower in her hair and amber necklace)*

Author's note

We do not hear any text in italics i.e. the phone conversations and **Alfie***'s thoughts.*

Act One

Scene One

Spring. Battered-looking flowers in flowerbeds to the back, maybe a table and a chair, implying external and internal spaces. Wooden boxes, drawers on stage for all props.

Young Beth (*the musician*) *introduces, welcomes and starts to play.*

'Lucky Star'

All through the days
And all through the years
Same way same kind
Same old sun

All through the days
And all through the years
Same world, same want
Same job done

Laugh until we cry
Storm in and out of every room
Talk late into the night
Counting each and every lucky star

All through the days
And all through the years
There's no other
Happiness but you

All through the days
And all through the years
We smile and we curse
And we shine through

Laugh until we cry
Storm in and out of every room
Talk late into the night
Counting each and every lucky star

All through the days
And all through the years
Same way same kind
Same old sun

All through the days
And all through the years
We smile and we curse
And we shine

Laugh until we cry
Storm in and out of every room
Talk late into the night
Talk late into the night

Laugh until we cry
Storm in and out of every room
Talk late into the night
Counting each and every lucky
Every lucky
How we're lucky,
Star

As Song is finishing, **Beth** *enters. She is furious. She shoots a grim
'look' at* **Young Beth** *and the audience, who reacts by finishing the
song abruptly and quickly putting her guitar down.*

Beth   And he went. (*Bitter abrupt laugh.*)
After twenty years.
Just.
Like.
That. Out of the door, suitcase packed
and gone.

Young Beth *reacts (maybe looks guilty for playing something so
happy, perhaps nervously picks up her guitar again, maybe a playful
moment as the force of* **Beth**'s *outrage rises), and then changes as*
Young Beth *does not sing but plays FX sound of a mobile ring.*

Beth *responds by picking up the phone.*

Beth (*on phone*)   Yes, it is. (*Beat.*) Thanks for ringing back.

You've found a crow?

Yes, I found it today?

In your garden?

Yes.

And it can't fly.

No.

Do you know if it was a car, or slammed into a window?

No, I don't know what happened to it.

Is it in shock? It could just be shock?

Yes. Well. It's afraid certainly. I don't know what do to with it? I guess it probably is in shock.

And it can't fly?

No.

Do you think its wing's broken?

Yes, it looks broken. I'd say so. Yes.
Rather than shock.

Can you tell if it's a young bird, a juvenile?

No, I've no idea what age it is, it could be teenage I suppose. I don't think it's old, I don't think it's age. No, I think the wing's broken.

Well, the best thing to do is to put it out of its misery.

Really? I don't think I can do that.

Well, that's the best advice. It's unlikely to recover.

Beth (*slightly annoyed*)   I Googled it and well, that's not what Wikipedia said.

Well, that's what I'm saying.

But according to Wikipedia there's a chance . . .

A small one.

Isn't that as good one as any?

Well, that's my advice as a vet. You can bring it in if you like, and I can put it down.

What?

Where do you live?

Alfie *enters slowly from the side, ambling, with crow head on.*

In the middle of nowhere. I've just moved from London.

Well, if you can get to me I'll put it down.

Can't you come to me?
Don't vets have a call out thingy?

Not for a crow. No, you can bring it to me and I'll put it down for you.

But you're miles away.

You risk killing the animal outright by moving it of course, especially if it's a long drive.

Beth *(now really annoyed)*   Right. So you suggest not moving it?!

Like I said, we recommend the best thing is to terminate its life.

I don't think I can kill a crow.

Well, really you should get a vet to do it.

But you think it will die if I drive it to you anyway.

Possibly.

Right. (*He's not been any help.*) Thanks.

Good luck with that then.

Yeah.

Beth *takes the mobile from her ear, the call is over.*

Beth *observes* **Alfie** *and then approaches, this terrifies him and he flaps limping and desperate holding his arm as she approaches.* **Beth** *approaches again with the same results.*

Silence. **Alfie** *breaths with fear. He is intensely vulnerable.* **Beth** *does not know what to do.*

When she finally speaks, she talks with great gentleness and very unlike the brisk person we met on the phone.

Alfie . . .

Beth   Well, it doesn't look good.

Alfie . . .

Silence.

Beth   You may never fly again.

Alfie . . . (*Yes, there is, humans normally kill birds.*)

Beth   I don't know what to do with you.

Alfie . . . (*Leave me alone.*)

Beth   I don't really want to look after a crow.

Alfie . . . (*Please leave me alone.*)

Beth (*to self*)   No.

Silence. **Beth** *still and* **Alfie** *terrified.*

Beth   These are words aren't they. You don't understand words.

Alfie . . .

Beth   Well, I won't come near then but, well . . . I could get you some food, I suppose, something to eat.
Worms I suppose. Yes, worms.
Don't be afraid, really don't be. There's no need to be, well only of the world I suppose, the whole of it.
(*Suddenly terribly sad.*) It's a pretty
rotten terrifying place actually
for anything wounded.

Silence and then, utter change of mood. . .

Goodness, I'm talking to it! That's
how bad things are!

Alfie . . .

Beth *shakes her head.*

Beth   Worms.

Scene Two

Montage – with music. Time passing. Summer ends.

a. **Beth** *attempts to give water to* **Alfie**. **Alfie** *is still afraid of her.
She fails.*

b. **Beth** *attempts to put* **Alfie**'s *wing in a sling. He won't be touched
by her and backs off.* **Alfie** *remains afraid of her.*

c. **Beth** *feeds* **Alfie** *worms (giant edible gummy worm sweets).* **Alfie**
is suspicious of her but hungry, eventually eats.(Funny.) **Alfie** *feels
less afraid.*

d. **Beth** *gives* **Alfie** *water again – he drinks.* **Alfie** *begins to trust
her.* **Beth** *begins to think he's cute.*

e. **Beth** *puts* **Alfie**'s *wing into a sling.* **Alfie** *is calm with her.*

f. **Beth** *gardens, not quite knowing what to do.*

g. **Alfie** *follows* **Beth** *as she moves about the garden. She doesn't
realize this at first and this makes her smile. It's the first smile we've
seen.*

h. *They play a game with her moving and him following. She can't
quite believe it. Real joy.*

i. **Beth** *gardens again.* **Alfie** *nearby.*

Young Beth

'What You Do To Me Now'

How can I get you to see me boy
Do you even know that I'm there
How can I get you to see me boy
What do you do to me now
I look, you look away
You look, I do the same
We look and we can't look away

What do you do to me now
What do you do to me now

Will you be mine, will you be my life line
Will you be mine,
I say you say, will you be mine

I wait, I wait for the phone to ring
I wait till night comes fast again
I watch the phone till half past ten

And then
What do you do to me now
And then
What do you do to me now
You ring!

Would you be mine, would you be my life line
Would you be mine, would you be my life line
Would you be mine

I say you say
I say you say

And we begin

And you say
I say you say
I say you say
You say I say
Yes!

Beth   What are you, a toddler, a teenager? Twenty, twenty-five, twenty-eight? No, you'd be dead then wouldn't you.

I wondered how long crows live?

Alfie . . .

Beth   I mean twenty-five in crow years. You've moved in, haven't you.

Alfie   . . . (*Yes, obviously.*)

Beth   Did I agree to you moving in? I don't remember there being a discussion. Usually there's a long discussion over commitment, not that I can really remember. I wrote a song once about moving in. I used to write songs.

Beth *suddenly appears inordinately sad – remembering. Introduction to Song begins.* **Alfie** *reacts to her sadness by doing something silly. She smiles again.*

Beth *continues to attempt to garden as song continues.*

Beth   Alfie. I'm going to call you Alfie.
How does that sound?

Alfie *looks blank.* (*He is a girl.*)

Young Beth

'Moving In'

Don't even have a table
Don't even have a bed.
Eating on the dusty floors
While the paint is wet

You've never held a hammer
You've never used a brush
You in your brand new overalls
You've left lumps in the gloss

Our first home, our first moving in
Stretches before us on the wooden floor.

The key turns the lock
As you turn in from the street
I hear you walking up the stairs
The third step creaks.

Hang your coat on the door
It's late you think I'm asleep
But I'm curled up in bed
And I'm waiting for you

(Repeat) Our first home, our first moving in
Stretches before us on the wooden floor
In unhung blinds and walls to paint
A house of open hearts, a house of open doors.

Scene Three

Beth *is attempting a different aspect of gardening – it goes wrong,*
eventually giving up and burying the whole thing? (Funny.) **Young**
Beth *plays FX sound of a mobile ring.*

Beth   It's from my sister, yet another helpful text.
Shall I read it?

Alfie *isn't listening.*

'One day "the Buddha"' (**Beth** *loudly sighs.*) 'met a woman
whose child had died'. (*She reads the text more like a shopping list*
or recipe than a story, quickly and with utter indifference
throughout.) 'She was wandering about in a' what? Oh yeah,
'a grief-stricken daze holding the tiny body. "Please give me
some medicine to save my baby," she begged . . .' I can't
pronounce that, Shak-ya-muni, is that the buddha? Is that a
type of noodle?

Alfie *starts hiding things as she continues.*

'He told her to fetch him some poppy seeds so he could
make medicine to save her baby, though the baby was
already dead, but only to accept poppy seeds from families
who had never known loss or bereavement. The woman
visited every household to ask. But although many had
poppy seeds.' (*To self.*) I don't have any poppy seeds! 'There
was not a single house in which there had never been a
death. The woman gradually came to realize that every

family had lost loved ones. Through this experience she
realized she was not alone in her feelings of grief.' Did that
help her, you have to ask?!

Putting the mobile away in irritation, switching it off.

Beth (*with irritation to* **Alfie**)   I know. Older sisters!

Beth *goes to collect the gardening tools. Everything has been moved
by* **Alfie**. *She collects them without realizing this is what he has been
doing,* **Alfie** *steals a garden tool, placing it on the other side of the
space.*

Alfie *is then caught with a garden tool in his hand, a purple-
handled trowel.*

Beth   What are you doing?

Alfie *keeps hold of it.*

Drop it. Drop it.
What are you thinking when you're doing that!
Drop it.
Is this adolescent defiance or are you just being a boy?
Alfie!

Alfie *doesn't drop it.* **Beth** *runs at him* **Alfie** *is terrified by the
sudden movement and panics again reverting to fear and drops it.*

Sorry. Sorry.
It's my sister and her holy, holy advice, always . . .
Sorry.

Beth *moves towards him and he backs off again.*

I'm really sorry.
He bought that. (*Referring to the garden tool.*) When we moved
here. I hate purple. It's an old lady's colour. The colour of
the spinster or divorcee.

What are you thinking?

Alfie *scolds her.* (*A set of consecutive caws.*)

What's that then?

Alfie *scolds.*

'Old bag' mmh?
Or the Buddha is dead.
Or purple.
Poppy seed.
TV.
Nonsense. I.

Alfie *scolds.*

Saturday Live.
Strictly Ballroom.
OLD BAG! OLD BAG!
Unwanted.
Or:

'Your grief overwhelms you like an ice-pick through the
your heart.
This I know, I know, I know
And this pain will never end.
Old bag
Strictly
Graham Norton.
Broad carpet.'

Sorry to shout.

Beth *goes to pick it up.* **Alfie** *grabs it before she can reach it, he then moves away with it in his hand, manoeuvring out of the way, as she approaches. This time it makes her laugh.*

Alfie *moves it to the furthest place he can and repeatedly caws at her – cackling, waddling and raising his legs up and down.*

Alfie *cackles.*

Alfie *makes her laugh. FX music and movement section. Section completed.* **Beth** *goes 'inside'.* **Alfie** *follows her.*

FX **Young Beth** *text tone.* **Beth** *picks up the phone and looks at it.*

Beth   My sister again.

Beth *considers texting and then does not as* **Alfie** *heads towards a brightly-coloured framed picture of a song bird and writing in reflective gold. It is an award, saying WINNER FOR BEST ORIGINAL YOUNG SONG WRITER OF THE YEAR 1998.*

No.

Alfie *moves towards it.*

No!

Alfie *moves towards it again.*

Alfie   . . .

Beth   NO!

It's very precious.

Alfie   . . . (*So what.*)

Beth *picks it up.*

Beth   It was the only time I've ever won anything. (*Reading it.*) 'Young Songwriter of the Year 1998'.
I used to play. I wrote love songs mainly. For him.

Pause.

Sang them too. Did concerts back in the day.
I've some photos somewhere. I wore flowers in my hair
and always my lucky green top for 'creativity and renewal'.
Oh and an amber necklace, it was supposed to create
balance,
and stuff, ease stress and protects, or some such rubbish.
(**Young Beth** – *dressed in this* – *looks down at her clothes,
fiddles with the necklace as it is referred to.*)
Beth   It's tree resin isn't it, ancient and from the wood.
The preserved past.
I lost it years ago.
It was a terrible look. Everyone else was into jeans and
trainers. (**Young Beth** *looks sad rather than offended.*)
I lost the necklace years ago, (*Wistful.*) on holiday, the cord
broke, I didn't realize until we got back to the hotel, it was
on the way back, from the lighthouse. We went back and

looked, but I never found it again. It's on our island, my necklace.

Beth *drifts off.*

But (**Beth** *suddenly looking at* **Young Beth**, *bitter.*) that person is dead now, the girl I was, sealed in the past. But I can still hear those stupid songs, going round and round in my head, charting our dead love, our happiness, (*Drifting.*) our summers.

Music intro to song. **Beth** *puts award back.*

Young Beth

'The Summer Song'

The sun burnt sands
Of warm summer days and nights
And sun charred leaves
That lie on dusty lanes

The tumbling hours
As long as fleeting shadows
We sit and watch
The deep and even sky

Two summer song birds
Sing to the lone island sun
Two summer song birds
Fly away when the song is done
Done

The evening gathers in
The moon it is unraveling the hours
Our precious hours
The ocean's rising tide
Edging on the quay

Drifting into sleep
Dreaming endless summer
Dreaming you, always you
Flotsam scattered forgotten
Resting by the blue

Two summer song birds
Sing to the lone island sun
Two summer song birds
Fly away when the song is done
Done

Two summer song birds
Sing to the lone island sun
Two summer song birds
Fly away when the song is done
Done

If only we could stay like this
If only we could make time still
O those summer song birds
Will soon fly away back home
Home

Beth *gets ready to go out shopping, putting on coat, finding purse, getting hessian shopping bags, deciding on how many to take etc.*

Alfie *watches her.*

Song finishes.

Alfie *moves towards the award again.*

What did I say.

He goes for it again, she grabs it off him.

I'll get rid of you.

Does something silly.

No don't make me laugh.

FX knock at the door. They both stop what they are doing. **Beth** *ignores it. A further knock at the door.* **Beth** *still ignores it.* **Young Beth** *slides a piece of paper towards her. She hands it back to the* **Young Beth** *who reads.*

Young Beth   Hi, Beth. How are you settling in?

Beth   Settling in.

Young Beth   It's always nice to have newcomers.
I hear you have a pet crow.

Beth *and* **Alfie** *exchange a look.*

Young Beth   I'm a bit of a birder myself.

Beth   I'm not a birder.

Pause.

And anyway I'm not staying. I'm selling the house, aren't I?
Can't she see the sign up? We only moved here because he
grew up here in this middle-of-nowhere-country-shit-place.

Beth *indicates that the* **Young Beth** *should continue.*

Young Beth   We're raising funds for the village hall.

Beth (*with contempt*)   Village hall!

Young Beth   And we wondered if you'd like to present a
talk about your crow, to help raise funds.

Beth (*to* **Alfie**)   What?

Young Beth   Perhaps I could come round to discuss it
with you?

Beth *scoffs.*

Beth   There's no point in making friends if you're moving,
is there! We lived in a flat the size of a pinhead in London;
can you imagine what half the money will get me now?
Something in Chingford or Penge West for Christ's sake.

Pause. **Beth** *indicates that the* **Young Beth** *should continue.*

Young Beth   Warm wishes.
Meg O'Brian.

Alfie   (*That's a 'no' then.*)

Beth   Of course it's no.

Young Beth *unsure of what to do, shares a look with* **Alfie** *and*
Beth *and then screws up the paper and drops it on the floor.*

Beth *grunts, picks up the empty hessian shopping bags and exits.*

Young Beth *and* **Alfie** *share a look.*

Scene Four

Music.

Alfie *on his own with the audience. Clearly bored.*
Goes to the audience and takes a shoe off.
Puts it on the other side of the stage.
Does the same with a coat or hat.
(This should be comical.) He repeats this several times, taking various items.
When audience is all laughing, **Beth** *enters. Into Scene Five.* **Alfie** *immediately stops what he has been doing.*

Scene Five

Beth *carrying full shopping bags and clearly distraught and furious, planting the bags down in the middle of the space. She sighs with irritation at* **Alfie.**

Alfie   . . . ?

Beth *gets out some whiskey, pours a shot and drinks.*

Beth *(sarcastic)*   Fancy one? Oh, I forgot you don't drink.

Alfie   . . . *(I do actually, whiskey's my favourite.)*

Alfie *continues to stare.*

Beth   It's alright for you.

Alfie   . . . *(Like what did I do?)*

Beth *(bitter)*   A bird, a bird doesn't have to even think about being or place or belonging! Does it! Do you!

Alfie   . . . *(Course not, I'm no navel gazer, none of us crows are.)*

Beth   I bet you don't even get time, do you.
Time?! Time, what's that! Eh, time! Monday, Tuesday,
Wednesday, a month, a year, a life time. Twenty years.
Twenty years, what a waste of my life.

She drinks and scoffs.

Alfie   . . . (*I understand time in a way that you cannot possibly
comprehend – you human, you!*)

Beth   I should just leave, I should just go. I should just go
and rent a place, until this is sold. Just head on back. It's just
money. I'll just get in debt. But then I'm already in debt,
aren't I?
Because this waste of space house cost so much.
And I gave up my job to come here. So I'm stuck, waiting to
sell it, no point in finding a new job. Just stuck. While he . . .
while he . . .

FX sound of a mobile ring. **Beth** *looks at her mobile.*

It's my sister again. (*To mobile.*) I don't want any more advice!

*She drinks again. She is now clearly very upset about something.
Silence before it all comes out. She is terribly hurt.*

I saw them. That's what.
I saw them all together.
Her, him and her kids.

Alfie   . . . (*Who?*)

Beth   The woman he left me for.
Her children and him and her, looking like a family.
Looking like they've always been. Like they always existed.
Looking like that. Like a family.

They were next to cake ingredients in Tesco's.
They were opposite preserves, just before you reach eggs.
That's where they were.

They didn't see me.
A family, a real family. Already. The other life, looking like
it's always been.

As if our time together never happened.
As if her kids were his.
And I'm a never been.

FX mobile. **Beth** *ignores it. Mobile goes off again.*

Beth *angrily picks it up.*

I DON'T WANT ANY MORE ADVICE ABOUT SEEDS!
Oh, sorry I thought you were my sister.

It's Meg, did you get my note?

Hello, Meg. Yes:

Did you get my note?

Yes, I got your note.

Will you do the talk?

No, I can't really.

It would be just wonderful if you could.

I just . . .

Please think about it.

I wouldn't know what to say

Haven't you read up on them.

What?

Crows.

Yes, I suppose a little, since Alfie.

Alfie, is that what you call him?

Yes. I gave him a name.

That's a great name.

Yes.

You sure it's a boy?

I think it's male. It behaves like one.

I think it's hard to tell.

In crows? Really?

It's really hard.

I've never really thought about it, I mean how you tell.
He's just so naughty. I sort of . . .

You must have so many stories about him now?

Yes, he is quite a character. But I really don't know much
about them. I've only looked them up on Google. And well, I
did order a few books but I haven't read them. I meant to.

That's wonderful.

Look, I don't want to seem rude but I'm not staying anyway.

Aren't you?

No.

Well, even so it would be brilliant to have you give a talk.

Meg . . .

Would be so brilliant.

Meg . . .

Such a great story to tell.

Meg!

Sorry.

I really don't know very much about crows.

*That doesn't matter. Just how it's been with Alfie would be so
interesting.*

Look, I'm sorry.

Well, just think about it, would you? It would mean so much.

Alright. I'll think about it.

Thank you, Beth, and if you ever want a coffee or a tea.

A coffee?

Or the pub.

The local pub?

Yes, for a drink? If you drink?

Yes, I drink.

Well, that's good then.

But I'm not staying.

That doesn't matter, it would be nice anyway.

Would it?

Of course it would, I'm just a few doors down. Must be a bit lonely. . .

I'll let you know.

The offer is always there, Beth.

Like I said, I'll let you know, Meg and. . . thank you.

Bye then.

Bye.

Beth *puts the mobile down, touched by the call and then changing her mind. Pause and then quietly to self.*

So they can laugh at me.
Of course, that's why they want me to do it.
Everyone knows, don't they.
They all know he's left me for his 'childhood sweetheart'.
Maybe that's why he wanted to move here
in the first place. Back to his village.
They want me to do the talk so they can all check me out.
I must be top gossip.

In a city, no one cares.
No one knows.

Maybe I'm cursed. Sometimes I think I'm cursed and have to pay back for all the happiness I ever had.

Maybe it's your fault. (*To* **Alfie**.)
You're a 'harbinger of doom', you know. I read it on
Wikipedia so it must be true, 'a harbinger of doom'.

Alfie   . . . (*A what?*)

Beth   Corvids are flesh eaters, carrion. You know you're a
corvid? Your speciality is cemeteries.

Alfie   . . . (*What are they?*)

Beth   You hang about them, that's right,
waiting to feed on the dead, to gloat, like the village.
To gloat and eat upon me.

Alfie   . . . (*You don't half talk some rubbish.*)

Alfie *clearly bored stops listening and begins pecking at something.*

Beth   Ugly, aren't you, close up. Like everything.
Harbingers of doom. And what was the other thing I read,
'a conductor of souls', all corvids. You accompany the hero
down to hell.

Alfie   . . . (*Get a grip?*)

Beth   I guess that's where I am. You reach a stage where
everything's loss, the future is one big just loss. Everyone
goes, dies or fucks off.

Alfie *bored again.*

FX music.

Beth *unpacks her shopping.*

Beth *talks as she unpacks.*

I dreamt I was you last night, I was inside you, stood on the
window ledge, spread out my wings, and flew, flew through
the summer air, across the pitch black field, over the church,
the pub, the Spar, to the other side of the village to him.
Flew into their new life, through the open window, up the
stairs and into their room. I saw them, lying curled round
each other . . . I saw them.

FX music intro to 'Abundance'.

(*Desolate.*) Make me a wolf, a wild boar, a bear, a winter
bear, an angry winter bear who's lost its soul mate.
An angry bear who will wait next to cake
ingredients, opposite the preserves and just before eggs,
wait until they walk past, and then
pounce, seize their white necks, sink my claws
into their throats and toss them gently into the cheese aisle –
or I might simply kill one of them, not both, leaving the
other to grieve, so they can share
this,
my mundane and average tragedy.

That has laid my life bare.

Make me an animal.

(*To* **Alfie**.) I won't eat you.
Even though a bear would eat a crow, if it could.

Alfie   . . . (*I think I'm going off you.*)

Beth   The other life. Their other life. Bet he'll take, take
her to our island, where we always holidayed. He'll walk up
to the lighthouse, our lighthouse, and back, go for tea in the
hotel café, where they'll have cheesecake or lemon meringue
pie, then they'll go back to the hotel room. . . And later
they'll have dinner in our hotel, where Filipe and Francesco,
the waiters, won't mention me. So it will be as if I was never
there either and their time was always there, running
alongside our fake life, and the real life, his real life, was with
her and never with me, not ours.

Young Beth

'Abundance'

Sky turned red
World was still
We walked down the hill
All seen all done

The heart grows quiet with age
The lines of your eyes
The lines of your hands

Always Always Always Always

Book well read
A path well shared
This bed is made
Of wandered moons
I'll hold you
In this moon beam
In this ever been
In this ever will

Always, Always, Always, Always

The clouds are closing in
The sky is heavy and the ocean turns
With brimming cold

One hundred moons
Two thousand suns
Love lies before
Love lies behind
All and ever been

The sky turned red
The world was still
We walked down the hill
All seen all done

Give me the open sky
And we'll speak in quiet hidden dust
Our secret words of love and lust

Always Always Always Always

I hold your steady soul
As if you were a hundred calling birds
This ever been this ever will

Always Always Always Always you

We are forever more
We walk into our hundred moons
We walk into our thousand suns
Into abundance
Into abundance

Beth *listens and maybe quietly cries.* **Alfie** *finds a piece of broken glass (maybe something to scare off crows) and attempts to give it to* **Beth**. **Beth** *still does not notice.*

Beth (*To self.*)   Don't! don't! (*Interrupting song.*)

I can't hear them. I won't hear those songs
Anymore. They can't be sung.
They won't be sung.
They mean nothing. They have no place.
No. Nothing.

Beth *exits. She still has not noticed the shiny glass.* **Alfie** *despondently moves it about the table and then turns to talk directly to the audience.*

He takes off his crow head, and sighs, a very human sigh, turns to the audience and smiles and then speaks.

Alfie   So migration. Let's talk about quantum entanglement.
This is the ability for two entwined particles moving away from each other to stay connected so that even at opposite ends of the universe if you alter one the other will immediately and identically be affected.
Many animals, you too in fact, possess a protein called cryptochrome, it is this chemical that reacts with the blue ray spectrum from the sun within the eye of a bird, that releases these two entwined particles. They spin away from the bird, measuring the magnetic field of the planet as they do so, over vast distances, whilst still connected to each other and informing me. Einstein dismissed it as 'spooky action'. But not anymore, like much of the weird world of quantum mechanics, and such ideas as multiple universes, similar and yet slightly different, quantum entanglement though

perhaps not yet fully understood by your species has been proven. These two particles are, you might say, outside of time, moving faster than light, so much so that you cannot say which is ahead in time and which is behind, they exist instantaneously, guiding me as I migrate. Something very clever that I can do, and you, well you, you really can't.

Alfie *caws and puts his head back on and is about to exit, maybe even leaves, leaving the performance space empty for slightly too long a time. He re-enters, head off.*

Oh, I forgot this is the interval. It'll be fifteen minutes, or will it, fifteen minutes in this time dimension but maybe twenty or even twenty-three in another.

Alfie *exits.*

Young Beth *gets up and returns the items taken from the audience by* **Alfie***, ad-libbing and apologizing for* **Alfie** *as she does so and then adding . . .*

Young Beth   No, it really will be fifteen minutes.

Interval.

Act Two

Scene One

It is autumn. All the flowers have gone, the flower beds are bare.
Young Beth *enters, followed by* **Alfie**. **Alfie** *climbs the ladder and
scatters leaves across the stage.*

Young Beth

'This Is It For Me'

Don't leave me love
Don't leave me
Breaking on my own tonight
Don't leave me love
For when you go I know I'll never
For when you go I know I'll never
This is it for me

Just tell me what I said
Tell me what I did
To let this slip

It can't just be your heart
Turning away
From all of this

I would do anything
Break everything
Burn it all down
Down to the ground
Just for you
To need me again

Don't leave me love
Don't leave me
Breaking on my own tonight
Don't leave me love
For when you go I know I'll never

For when you go I know I'll never
This is it for me

I'm sick
Sick to the stomach
Dreaming of you

I'm lost
In the raging sea
For you

The birds are gone
This barren heart
Is turning over, sleepless
Is it something that I said
Is it something that I did
Please don't let this slip

Don't leave me love
Don't leave me
Breaking on my own tonight
Don't leave me love

For when you go I know I'll never breathe again
For when you go I know I'll never breathe again
This is it for me

Young Beth *is reaching the end of the song. Repeating the chorus*
Beth *enters with binoculars and trowel and scowls at* **Young Beth**
who immediately stops and then mouths the words.

Young Beth   Sorry.

Alfie *hops down and starts to follow* **Beth**. **Alfie**'s *sling is off.* **Beth**
plants some bulbs. **Alfie** *watching, head resting on one side as he*
observes her, bored. When **Beth** *has finished planting she picks up*
the binoculars and looks skyward, speaking with them held to her
eyes.

Beth   Thought I'd, you know. (*Referring to binoculars.*) Try it.

Alfie   . . . (*What on earth are you doing?*)

Beth   It's called birding. Watching birds.

Alfie   . . . (*Why would anyone want to do that?*)

Beth   I don't expect you to understand Alfie. (*Speaking as she looks through them.*) You've inspired me in away.
Wow, I think that's a dunnock, or is it a sparrow?

Alfie   . . . *Now bored* (*Big deal and what you can't tell the difference, and it is way more likely to be a sparrow, idiot!*)

Beth *continues to birdwatch.* **Alfie** *sits on the garden bed, he digs at the earth playfully to begin with, stopping to see if he has got* **Beth***'s attention yet, then chucking out more soil when he fails to do so, stopping again and waiting whilst* **Beth** *continues birding, finally he goes mad and hurls great wads of soil into the space.*

Beth *screams at him when she sees the mess he has created.*

Beth   What are you doing! I've just planted them and I've people coming round to see the house in an hour!

Alfie *stops. Looks at her. But he's having fun, so he just goes back to hurling soil.* **Beth** *runs at him, screaming.*

Alfie *flies* (*suggest this is beautiful – maybe just with his hands*).

Music.

Alfie *returns to the ground, exhausted catching his breath, breathing hard in and out. He has surprised himself but found flying very hard (he is not quite well yet). A moment as he catches his breath.*

Beth *is delighted – the happiest we have seen her.*

Beth   I was told you'd never fly again. Oh Alfie.
Wait, wait, I have to share this with someone.

Beth *picks up mobile*

Beth   No, not my sister.

Beth *picks clearly looks through a number of names.*

Who'd be interested anyway.
Where's that note.

She finds the note from Meg, then dials.

Hi. Is that Meg?

Yes. Who's this?

Beth, Beth Burton.

Alfie *is preening himself, admiring his arms (wings). Maybe upstaging!*

He flew?

Alfie?

Yes, yes.

Wow, that's fantastic. That's all you, looking after him.

Yes, I can't believe it. I was told he'd never recover.

How far did he fly?

Not far.

Well, he's probably still not completely recovered.

No. I guess that will take more time.
He'd just wrecked a flowerbed.

They can be really destructive

Don't I know it.

(Silence.)

Well, I'll leave you to get on, Meg. I just, well, I had to share it with someone, silly really, sorry to bother you.

It's such great news, I'm honoured that you rang me. (Beat.)

Well, see you.

What about that talk then?

The talk?

Go on, just while you're here, what harm can it do. Before you sell the house.

I don't know. I really don't know what I'd say.

Just talk about Alfie.

Well, yes, I suppose I don't have to be a crow expert.

I could just make it all about him. Though wouldn't that be rather dull for people?

No, the village would love to hear about that.

No, I don't think so.

Have you done much reading about them?

A little, to check that I was sort of doing it right.
I read one book which said you shouldn't let them identify with you too much, adopt them I suppose. It makes it harder for them to go back into the wild. But it's too late for that now. He follows me everywhere.

That's so interesting.

Is it? Is it interesting?

Yes.

I wouldn't want people to feel short changed.

So that's a yes?

Beth (*she laughs*)   No, that's not a yes.

But a maybe?

More of a maybe.

Still better than a no. What about drink, tonight? To celebrate.

Well. I don't know. It's not like Alfie can celebrate with us. I can't take him into the pub and anyway, I've some people coming round for a second viewing later.

A second viewing?

Yes, I think they're really interested. It's taking so long to sell.

After that then. They do great beer.

I don't really drink beer.

Great selection of wines too.

(Laughing at Meg's insistence but liking her.)

Yes, I drink wine.
We'll see. I'll ring you after.

Great.

Ok. Bye. *(Beat.)* Oh Meg! Meg! I'll need a place for Alfie, when I leave. I'll be moving into a flat. I don't suppose you . . .?

There's a crow sanctuary at Westonburt.

Right.

You could take him there.

An aviary? Far from here?

It's about fifteen miles. They help them to rehabilitate so they can be placed back in the wild.

Perfect.

I'm so excited that you might be doing the talk. It would be so interesting.

Yes.

When do you think you can let me know?

The thing is, you see, if I can be honest, Meg. I'm worried my ex will show up. That's really why I don't want to do the talk.
And his, you know his, his . . .

And Susan?

Yes, her.

They've gone away for a month I think.

A month! They've gone away for a month?! Do you know where?

To Malta.

Oh, we used to go there. (*Trailing off.*) There's a lighthouse that we used to . . .

So if you do it next week say, they definitely won't turn up.

Right.

So you will do it?

Can I let you know later?

Of course. And don't forget about the drink.

Yes. Bye, Meg.

Bye.

Beth *and* **Alfie** *exchange a look.* **Beth** *gets a broom and clears up the space, putting the earth back in the flowerbeds.*

Beth   You going to help me with this?

Alfie *bored again – might kick his feet.*

I didn't think so.

Young Beth *FX text tone.*

Beth   It's my sister again,

Alfie *carries on kicking his feet taking no notice of* **Beth**.

Beth   No I'm not talking to her. She's getting to the 'telling me off stage'. I should be over it by now apparently. Moved on. 'Get over it' as if your life is nothing more than an inconvenient fence.

Beth *holds up another bulb at* **Alfie**.

And this time it's staying in the ground?
Not that I'll ever see them.

She attempts to plant and then stops.

He's taken her to our place. He's taken her on holiday to our island. (*To self, quietly.*) Bastard.

Bastard.

Scene Two

Beth *is rehearsing her talk. Talking directly to us. She is reading from cards as a prompt.* **Alfie** *enters as she talks, bored and troublesome.*

Beth   'I have a crow. His name is Alfie.
What a lot of people don't know about crows is, one, how
bright they are and two, how much they like to play.
Alfie will hide things from me, move garden tools,
wellingtons even, anything that is light enough to move,
and crows are stronger than you think. Then I swear,
once he sees me looking and usually annoyed he caws,
as if laughing at me. How can a crow have a sense of
humour? They play, it's been recorded, in Russia there are
accounts of hooded crows, sledging using plastic lids. That's
a crow using a tool, well, a sledge, to play. They repeat this,
there is footage of this online, and they are clearly having a
ball. Humour and play, not something one imagines a bird
can experience. But these amazing birds do.

Crows or corvids, the family of birds they are from, are
exceptional amongst birds, and the brightest of them all.
And they bring gifts! I have a pile of gifts that Alfie . . .

Alfie *attacks a mug.*

Don't do that.
'Hello.' I should say my name. 'Thank you for having me',
That sounds very odd. 'I have a crow.'
Maybe I should start talking about birding, 'For me it's like
when time stops', no, that sounds really up myself.

Alfie *bored attacks something else, maybe a butter dish.*

Don't do that. I'm losing my place, Alfie.
'Hello, my name's is Beth Burton and I have a pet crow.'

Alfie *bored attacks something else.*

Stop it. What's got into you. Don't. Now where was I.
'Crows will have a sound or you could say a "name" for a
human they know.'

Alfie *goes for the certificate for the songwriting award.*

Put it down, put it down.

Alfie *drops it and it shatters.*

No!

Beth *tries to pick up the glass and cuts her fingers.*

Beth *screams at* **Alfie**. **Alfie** *does not care, he scolds at her and hops around the space (kitchen) in fury. She attempt to pick up the award again and cuts herself again.* **Alfie** *continues scolding.* **Beth** *shouts hysterically at him as he continues to scold and flap about.*

Stop it!
Stop it!

He has gone too far. Defeated she sits on the floor.

Alfie *pushes a mug to the edge of a the table (box) but* **Beth**, *defeated, does not react.*

Beth *picks up her mobile and dials a number, as she waits for answer she talks to* **Alfie**.

Beth   You know I'm leaving anyway.
You know that!
Is this Westonburt Aviary?

Yes.

I have a crow. I've nursed him back to health.
He can fly a little but not very far and he's slightly too acclimatized to humans I think.
He had a broken wing.
And anyway I don't think he'll survive in the wild. You see, I'm selling my house, going back to the city.
I've accepted an offer, so. I've just been putting it off really. (*This hurts.*) Would you take him?

Yes. Of course. That's what we're here for.

Great. Great. Thank you. (*Pause.*)
Shall I drive him over?

We're open till five today.

Today yes, that's sensible. Of course. Today.

See you later.

Thanks.

Bye.

Beth *ends the call. Looks at* **Alfie**. **Alfie** *does not understand what is happening.*

You're well. I mean.
They'll help you to get better. They'll rehabilitate you.
Help you to return to the wild. (*She knows this might not happen.*) But I've probably mucked that up too.

Beth *doesn't know what to do.* **Alfie** *doesn't understand.*

Music.

I'm sorry.

Hesitates and then slowly picks up **Alfie**'s *debris; finally picking up something that represents* **Alfie** *– maybe the first thing he stole – and puts it in a cardboard box.*

She picks the box up very gently, carrying the imagined bird inside.

Alfie *walks out of the space.*

Scene Three

Montage – with reprise of 'Abundance'. Time passing. Autumn.

a. **Beth** *tidies the garden.*

b. *Clears weeds from the boxes.*

c. *She puts everything away.*

d. *The last thing she puts away is the purple trowel.*

e. *She finds a black feather.*

f. *She sits sadly on her own, and shivers in the cold.*

g. *Leaves fall.*

Scene Four

Beth *is in the kitchen.*

Young Beth *FX sound of a mobile ringing.*

Beth *looks at the phone to see who is ringing her and then picks up the phone.*

Beth   Hi, sorry I haven't rung back, I meant to. It's been too long . . .

The caller goes berserk (it's her sister), forcing **Beth** *to take the phone away from her ear, every now and again she brings it back attempting to speak but is always shouted over. Bringing mobile back to her ear.*

Well, I . . .

Shouting continues. She takes the mobile away from her ear. A moment passes, she then brings mobile back to her ear.

No, that's not what Mum always said about me!

Shouting continues. She takes the mobile away from her ear. Bringing mobile back to her ear.

I . . .

Shouting continues. Taking it abruptly away, and almost immediately trying again.

No.

Shouting continues. Taking it abruptly away, and almost immediately trying again.

I did . . .!

Shouting continues. Taking it abruptly away, and almost immediately trying again.

No.

Shouting continues. Taking it abruptly away, and almost immediately trying again.

You can't say that . . .

Shouting continues. Taking it abruptly away, holding it nearer so she can hear the ranting but waiting some time before she places it near her ear again to speak once more.

Had it all? How can you . . .

Phone clearly goes dead. She puts mobile down, away from herself.

She sits on her own in the space for a moment and then exits. She might cry as wind picks up.

Into the storm.

Suggestions on how to depict: music, thunder sticks etc.

Movement – **Alfie** *and* **Beth**, *running about space, knocking everything over, stamping with feet and moving in rhythm.*

Scene Five

Beth *is in the garden, everything has been blown over. She is tidying up from the storm.*

FX **Young Beth** *mobile rings.*

Beth *picks it up.*

Beth   Hello.

This is Westonburt Aviary. Are you in the middle of something?

No, I'm just tidying up, after the storm. I'm fine to talk. How's Alfie?

That's why I'm ringing. I am afraid he's gone. The storm. It blew down his aviary. Your crow . . .

The storm? What, it blew down?

Yes. The aviary collapsed. Some of the birds were crushed.

They were crushed?! Alfie?

We don't know. Not for certain.

Right?

We're really sorry.

Right. (*Pause.*) So he might be dead? Is that what you're saying. Is that why you're ringing? Alfie's dead?

We just don't know. It was a terrible storm.

You don't know.

We're really sorry.

So you don't know if he's dead.

No.

But some did die.

Yes, we're sorry. Bye. It was a bad storm.

Yes.

Beth *is stunned by the news, near to tears. A moment passes.*

Young Beth   I am going to play something now.

Beth *looks up, shakes her head.*

Beth   Sixteen, I was sixteen.

Beth   In my lucky green top and amber necklace.
A flower in my hair.

Young Beth   With Anne.

Beth   My sister. Both of us.

Young Beth   Together we'd played for hours. Before him.

Beth   Before him.

Young Beth   Yes, before him. Before anyone.

Young Beth

'*My Sister*'

The sky is full of what could be's
Soaring high above the city park
We're on a rocket to the moon
We'll touch the stars before the night
Will hold each other's hand in flight
Will you still remember
Sister I'll remember

One of these endless days
We'll run away
In the heart of a star strung night
We'll run away

A two sister adventure
Climb a mountain too high
Cross the great a burning desert
Save the world every time
In the hour-glass of a moment
Leave the door wide open
One of these endless days
We'll run away

Song ends with silence.

Beth   I'm not that person anymore.

Young Beth   No?

Beth   No. And I still can't ring her. And Alfie's probably
dead
And, and everything, everything . . . (*She trails off.*)

Young Beth   You'll be late for the talk.

Beth (*to self*)   I'm not doing it.

Young Beth   Do you good.

Beth *shakes her head.*

Scene Six

A few hours later.

Beth *gets gradually more upset as she talks.*

Beth   Hello, thanks for coming.
That was quite a storm. I know trees fell down and
Some of you must have found it hard to get here.

I'm so, I have, had a pet crow.
Umm, as many of you know.
What you might not know is how bright they are.
They remember when you harm them, birds caught to be
ringed, or if you damage one, when they spot you again
they gather and scold you. Studies have found that not only
the original bird that you hurt, or let be hurt, scolds but all
their family and friends do also, they join in scolding.
Studies have shown that the original crow never forgets
and will scold you for years, even if you return to their
territory infrequently. And if you're kind to them they bring
you gifts, Alfie brought me gifts – a screwed ball of foil, a
bead, some flint, a feather, a small ball of coloured string.
(*She breaks down.*) Sorry. I. Would you excuse me. I had some
bad news earlier.
I . . . I . . . Excuse me.

Beth *leaves the space.*

Scene Seven

Beth *returns to the place of loss. She sits with an empty bottle of
wine, she gets up. She is drunk.*

Beth   Where are the completion documents. For the house?

Young Beth *hands her the documents.*

Beth *sits down and as she signs them.*

Young Beth *FX bleeps of a text.* **Beth** *ignores mobile.* **Young Beth** *FX bleep of another text. She looks at it and places them back on the ground. Bleep again.*

Beth   I can't read it.

Young Beth *takes the phone.*

Young Beth   It's your sister.
Shall I read it?

Beth *shrugs (if you like).*

Young Beth   Firstly please let me say I am so sorry to have shouted at you. I lost my temper, you have ignored me for so very long, and I was so upset. You texted me to tell me that your crow is dead and I am also so sorry for that.
On top of losing Matthew, that must be so very hard for you.
I know your crow brought a new lease of life to dark days.
I wanted to say this to you. This is what I meant to say rather than just shouting at you. I am content, you have often accused me of this, and yes I have been content for many years. I think you called me smug. But I know that I missed out on something in my life. There were no great loves, a couple of fumbles here and there, but no one of significance and there are no children, for you or I. But there is still warmth and food and comfort and friends, and in my case contentment. But you were loved so tremendously, he loved you and I know it resides in the past, Beth, but it still happened. It still happened. And please be happy for that – for the unloved, someone like myself, and my life, have never seen such abundance.

Beth *folds the documents and puts them in her jacket.*

Beth *continues to quietly garden. It snows.*

Beth *picks up the mobile and rings her sister.*

Beth   Hi, it's me. Sorry it's been so long.

Song ends.

Scene Eight

Beth *addresses the audience directly.*

Beth   My apologies for last time. I had just heard the news
that my crow, well Alfie, had died in the storm, his aviary
collapsed, he was crushed, they think.
So my bird, my crow, Alfie.

Let's start with some surprising facts about crows.
Nearly all crows have been observed using tools. Give them a
jar with some food at the bottom of it and a hook and a
bright crow will scope the food out with the hook dangling
from his beak.
Many stay in family units, continuing to support and learn
from each other. They are very social, thriving in family
groups.
They are very brave, they frequently mob hawks and eagles,
any birder will have seen that, and they are known to drop
sticks or even stones on anything deemed a predator, and
that includes us.
Crows can be taught to speak, especially the raven. Dickens
had a pet raven he called Grip, if you've read *Barnaby Rudge*,
you'll know that one of the main characters is a raven. He
taught Grip to say: 'Keep up your spirits,' 'Never say die,'
and 'Polly put the kettle on. Let's all have tea.' Dickens and
his family were so sad when Grip died early that they had
the bird stuffed and you can still see Grip at the Free Library
of Philadelphia, the bird's final resting place.
Crows have the most remarkable memory. They move their
stash of food up to as many as three times, remembering
exactly where it is on each occasion.
They have the largest brains of all birds apart from parrots.
Their brain to body ratio is not far off human proportions.
Crows occasionally kill each other. No one knows why.
Though I never saw any homicidal tendencies in Alfie.
Though he could be exceptionally irritating.
Crows mate for life and are monogamous, parting only in

death. Though the male sometimes wanders, so no surprises there. (*She smiles – this is NOT loaded.*)

They do migrate, though some are resident, they migrate by as much a thousand miles, normally to warmer climes.
One of my favourite stories, and I do hope this is true, concerns the famous animal behaviourist and Nobel laureate Konrad Lorenz who had a pet crow, which came home one day limping, and when Lorenz instinctively said: 'What happened to you?' he was startled when the bird replied 'Got my leg caught in a bloomin' trap.' But in German of course.

But let's go back to migration.
And this is where it gets really interesting.
We know birds respond to the magnetic field of the planet, but what we have been unable to work out is how they apply that to the vast distances some of them fly.
What we now know is that they use a technique called quantum entanglement, throwing out two electrons in opposite directions, that continue to inform each other and then relay information instantaneously back to the bird.
There is no way of knowing which particle is ahead in time and which is past.
They both exist in the same moment.

Memory as we know is very subjective, but the notion that through our understanding of quantum mechanics and certainly quantum entanglement that our moments from the past co-exists, well that's a thought and a half.

I often wondered how Alfie saw time. Did he see it as an un-separated thing, if you experience the past and the future in one moment then perhaps for him there was neither or always both, simultaneously.

He inspired me to view time differently, to observe as he observes, as he gathers information from these two spinning electrons, miles apart, in time and space, through the eye of a bird.

She stops, puts down her notes. Pauses. Drifts away.

Music underscores. It is as if she is speaking to herself rather than to the audience, she is perhaps back home even.

Now we are standing in my favourite place, it is an island, surrounded by a warm sea, and I am walking down from the lighthouse, the light is going and we have three more days left on the island and we will go to the hotel café now, have a pot of tea and he will have cheesecake and I will have lemon meringue pie, and we'll steal from each other's plates, while the other is reading. Then we will go to our sea-view room and do what couples do, and it won't be like it was when we first met but it will still be good. And then we will sleep for a little, and then we'll shower, and then we'll both over-dress for dinner and in the hotel restaurant Filipe and Francesco, who always remember us, will serve us, and joke, and we will order the local light white wine, our favourite. And all of that is ahead and we both know that it's ahead in time, as we walk down the hill from the lighthouse.

Some people never have a moment of such abundance.

Pause.

And ahead there are the endless moments of now.
And all the people you are yet to meet.
And in the eye of a bird, I think maybe they all of happen at once.

Because right now, at this very moment, somewhere, I am walking down from the lighthouse, and everything for us is still ahead, and we are walking into abundance.

Clapping started by **Young Beth**. *Into music.*

Scene Nine

Beth *picks up mobile and taps to call up a number. She waits for the call to be answered.*

Beth   Hi. It's me.

Hi.

So, I'm going to buy you out.

Have you got enough to do that?

No. But I'll find it.

I'm surprised you want to stay.

Well, I do.

Oh.

Beth (*beat then she laughs*)   I'm not staying because of you.

Aren't you?

No. I'm staying because I guess because, something about that crow I had. Something. Maybe I feel I belong even, if that doesn't sound too odd. Sometimes you just connect with a place, don't you.

Of course.

If you don't mind?

No, of course I don't. I just want you to be happy, Beth.

And I want you to be happy, Matthew, truly, both of you.

Thank you, that means so much. I heard your talk was a hit?

Yeah, it went really well. Listen, I've got to get on. Meg's coming round to brief me on my new job.

Meg O'Brian?

Yes, I'm going to work for her. We've become quite close.

That's great.

And I want to finish some gardening before she gets here. My bulbs are coming up.

You gardening?

Yeah, people change, don't they.

(*Pause*) *Bye.*

Bye, Matthew.

Music: reprise of 'Summer Song'.

Scene Ten

Spring. **Beth** *is in the garden. The flowers have bloomed.*

She cannot find her shears. Then she cannot find her purple trowel.

She is confused by this.

Alfie *enters.*

She can't believe it.

Music.

Beth   Alfie? Alfie? Is that you? It can't be.

Is it? Alfie? It is?

Oh Alfie!

I thought you were dead . . . (*She cannot finish the word, she is overcome.*)

Alfie *gives her her trowel. She laughs, recovering. A moment.*

Where have you been? Where did you go?

Where have you been?

Alfie *is distracted. She misinterprets this.*

Beth   Oh Alfie, and I left you. I didn't know what to do. When I took you to the aviary. I'm so sorry. I didn't know. (*Once more overwhelmed.*)

Alfie *continues to be distracted. FX chicks.*

After a moment he produces, from his chest, five chicks.

Beth   They're yours.
You're a dad, a dad!

Where's the mum, then? Where's your lady?
Mrs Alfie. She near? No?

You're? (*Beat.*) They're? (*Beat. The penny drops.*)
They're yours, I mean, they're . . .
I mean, I mean. Alfie, you're a girl.
You're their mum.
Oh, you're a mum.

Beth *laughs with sheer joy.*

What life.

Alfie *caws with pride.* **Beth** *and* **Alfie** *play with the chicks, feeding them.*

Young Beth *and* **Beth**

'Lucky Star'

Beth *finally sings too.*

All through the days
And all through the years
Same way same kind
Same old sun

All through the days
And all through the years
Same world, same want
Same job done

Laugh until we cry
Storm in and out of every room
Talk late into the night
Counting each and every lucky star

All through the days
And all through the years
There's no other
Happiness but you

All through the days
And all through the years
We smile and we curse
And we shine through

Laugh until we cry
Storm in and out of every room
Talk late into the night
Counting each and every lucky star

All through the days
And all through the years
Same way same kind
Same old sun

All through the days
And all through the years
We smile and we curse
And we shine

Laugh until we cry
Storm in and out of every room
Talk late into the night
Talk late into the night

Laugh until we cry
Storm in and out of every room
Talk late into the night
Counting each and every lucky
Every lucky
How we're lucky,
Star